HIGHFIELD
A VILLAGE REMEMBERED

Text: John Edgar Mann

Research: Peter Ashton

HALSGROVE

First published in 1998 by Halsgrove
Copyright © 1998 John Edgar Mann and Peter Ashton

ISBN 1 874448 91 4

British Library Cataloguing-in-Publication-Data
A CIP data for this book is available from the British Library

*Front and back cover photographs:
Highfield Lane, Southampton, around the turn of the century.*

HALSGROVE
Halsgrove House
Lower Moor Way
Tiverton EX16 6SS
T: 01884 243242
F: 01884 243325
www.halsgrove.com

Printed and bound in Great Britain
by Hillman Printers (Frome) Ltd

Contents

	Acknowledgements	5
	Map of Highfield	6
	Introduction	7
1	Looking Back	9
2	Days of Elegance	11
3	'Nob Hill'	13
4	Death at the Uplands	15
5	'A Pretty Village Church'	16
6	A Village Church No Longer	19
7	Babbling Brooks in Shady Nooks	21
8	Residents of Roselands	23
9	A Link with a Rural Past	25
10	The Story of a Village School	28
11	Taunton's – the Name Lives On	32
12	Their Happiest Days? Perhaps...	36
13	The Portswood House Estate	39
14	Herbert Collins: A Man of Vision	41
15	When Horses Pulled the Trams	43
16	The Smell of Soap and Steam	45
17	Highfield in the First World War	47
18	Highfield in the Second World War	49
19	Pubs: East Side, West Side	54
20	Lodges and Other Survivors	57
21	Suburbanites at Their Leisure	60
22	Before the University	63
23	The University Today	66
24	A Highfield 'Who Was Who'	71
25	A Picture Miscellany	74
	Bibliography	80

*Dedicated
to the memory
of Highfield resident
Marjorie G. Bozie
(1916–96)*

Acknowledgements

Many people have given their time to help us in preparing a book that could easily have been twice as long as it is. They include Brian Ticehurst, Monica Brown, the Revd David James, Margaret (Patsy) Goodall, Leila Duffy, Jean Hawkins, Thelma Hallett, Gwen Jones, C.J. Knott, Peter Lewin, Peter Molsen, John and Julia Slade, Arthur Offer, Mollie Manns, Mrs D. Heasall, Mrs Penfold, Jill Neale, Mrs E. Wilson, Arthur Burns, Roger Bennett, Dr Richard Preston and his staff at the Southampton Reference Library, Sarah Watts of Southampton University, the library staff of the *Southern Daily Echo* and Sheila Ballantyne and Malcolm Nethersole of the *Echo*'s photographic department, and the staff of the Hampshire and Southampton Record Offices. We would also to thank Southern Newspapers plc for the loan of photographs and Alan Leonard for reading the manuscript and tendering his advice.

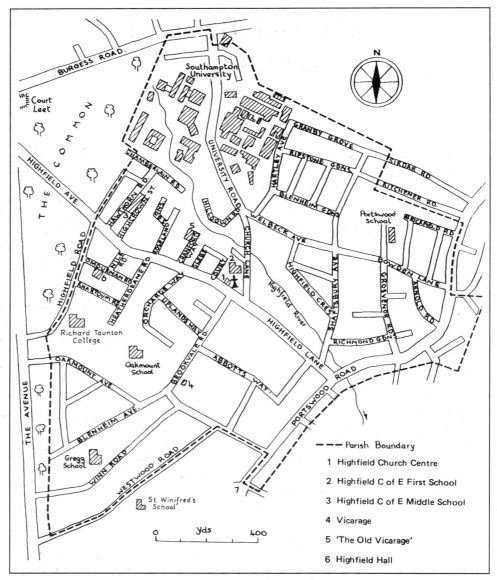

This interesting map, which appeared in a commemorative booklet by Martin Dedman entitled 'Highfield Church 1847–1977: A Story of Growth, Change and Development', shows that the boundaries of the parish are more extensive than many people imagine.

Introduction

by John Francis

Leafy, charming, cosy Highfield! Prim and proper Highfield? Well, yes, though lawless passion has been heard of, and it is saved from dullness by a different kind of conformity, the conformity of the student. Highfield is shot through with a strong flavour of the groves of Academe. Here we are slap in the middle of the University belt. No don billows by in a black silk gown, but around any corner one always might.

The boundaries are defined (see the map opposite) but Highfield, being partly a state of mind, resists pinning down. I always feel that outcrops of Highfield probably occur in Bassett. In Chilworth, however, never.

Even in April, the cruellest month, Highfield has an autumnal feel. Highfield would forgive the discovery of your paramour's strangled body in your Volvo; less easily overlooked would be the dressing of your whole garden with washday bunting on the Sabbath.

Perhaps Highfield is the answer Southampton makes to London's Hampstead. In terms of wealth and status Bassett has the edge but one can't help feeling that Highfield knows, with a touching if irritating certainty, that it is subtly better.

The quintessential Highfield car is a touch chic yet never flash, a car that expects to feel the warmth of the Tuscan sun on its bonnet at the right season. A dark-windowed BMW would not feel at home in Highfield. That there is wealth in Highfield seems certain, but its display, so usual with wealth elsewhere, is only fleetingly glimpsed. The money is sensibly and safely invested.

Tea may well be poured under the apple tree from old silver, but distinction and background are implied, not stated. No swimming-pools, no *dolce vita*, in Glebe Court or Orchards Way.

The gardens, with their shaved lawns, would not be big enough for kidney-shaped pools or comfortable with the flash of bronzed limbs (and, to be rather beastly, the limbs might not be that shapely). Highfield is inclined to be autumnal not only in mood; it is an area dominated by the elderly. The hearse is seen only a little less regularly than the milk float.

What saves Highfield, then, from being nice but dull? Pockets of resistance. Take Roselands Gardens, which has a villagey feel, or Omdurman Road, which has a brooding quality.

The prevailing wind blows from the left. This is *New Statesman* land; the *Guardian*, not the *Telegraph*, is read here. Lights burn late, so naturally morning curtains are drawn back late, too. Students leaven the slightly heavy quality. From one house you may catch the drift of a Scarlatti sonata and from the other the heavy industrial thump of more up-to-the-minute stuff.

Maintaining the village mood set by Roselands Gardens or Highcrown Street are the cluster of shops just before Highfield Lane runs out into the Common. For many years one shop had painted on a wall the encouraging slogan 'Our Aim Your Satisfaction'. How heartening to know this the first time you ventured inside to buy six rashers of smoked back bacon. You sensed, too, that you would be known by your second visit.

In Highfield you are pushed willy-nilly into a role.

You must be a feckless student, a mad poet, a dotty lecturer, a Bolshevik, a sweet old lady. A conspiracy confines you permanently to the role selected by Highfield Central Casting and play up to it you must.

The lower end of Highfield Lane peters out in a swampy delta of guest-houses, and houses where youths have clubs and dentists drill. It ceases to be Holy Highfield just below the church.

Highfieldishness, however, runs strongly uphill, even unto the Nuffield Theatre, which (after the church) is to Highfield what the Kremlin is to Holy Russia.

The top part of Brookvale Road and all of Abbotts Way are riddled with Highfieldishness *in excelsis*. The lower end? Not so sure.... We have to exclude Winn and Westwood Roads, of course; having gone down they have now gone up. The newish blocks of flats hint of Chilworth or even the best parts of Bournemouth. Having achieved devolution they are toying with independence.

There is much to be said for Highfield and little to be said against. But, just as when, walking up the Mall and seeing the Royal Standard over Buckingham Palace, one says to oneself, 'There will always be an England,' one has strong patriotic feelings on passing Highfield Church on Sunday (packed to the doors) and catching the sound of hymns being sung and, higher up the road, sniffing the roasting beef.

Vivat, vivat, Highfield!

1 – Looking Back

The 'Hayfield' of the old maps suggests a rural past, but then the environs of Old Southampton were nothing if not rural. You don't have to travel too far back in time to find farms, fields and grazing animals where leafy suburbia now flourishes.

At the centre of things was the village, and Highfield's can be pinpointed on the bend in Highfield Lane close to where the houses of the gentry looked out on the Common. Locals still regard it as their village, even though – and here is a sign of the times – the shops on the left-hand side of the road are, as we write, all boarded up, bar the barber's (many have chuckled at his Happy Families name: Mr Shearing).

The building of desirable residences has over the years given this local Hampstead a plush, posh feel. It wasn't always so. In the early years of the century there was a soup kitchen at Portswood School and between 150 and 200 impoverished families were listed to receive free soup.

Writing in a Southampton Local Studies Group publication in 1982, Dora Caton (b. 1915) recalled the weekly visits of the muffin man and the knife-grinder. And every Friday on the corner of Holyrood Avenue and Highfield Crescent a man with a barrel organ (and a monkey) played 'The Last Rose of Summer'.

In the memories of old-timers the name Sidney Kimber crops up often. Brickmaker, builder and local politician, his slogan was 'Vote for Kimber, who says what he means and means what he says.' He is remembered for his little blue car, almost the only one in Highfield at the time, and for his brickfield, on which now stands much of the University.

The field was a favourite playground for the local kids, and the alderman, aided by his faithful collie, could often be seen chasing them out. Jean Hawkins, who lived in Salisbury Road, told us: 'We used to go through a gap in our hedge and climb down the bank. There were two or three ponds with newts and tadpoles and loads of low bushes to make dens in.' Children made forts and look-outs with the bricks.

Also recalled is Sidney (later Sir Sidney) Kimber's habit of collecting rents before the working day had begun.

Thelma Hallett remembers milk from Pelham's dairy farm (behind her family home in Chamberlain Road) being delivered by means of a churn standing on a pram, and Gwen Jones describes how Mr Pelham used to walk his cows up to the Common and bring them home again in the afternoon.

The years rolled on, and Highfield inexorably changed from village to suburb, but many families

Thelma Hallett

Gwen Jones

stayed put. In 1937 the Rolphs celebrated a hundred years of one family in charge of Highfield Post Office. Interviewed by the *Echo*, postmistress Lily Rolph talked about a time when what is now Glebe Court was the Vicarage garden and the housing estates to the left of Highfield Lane were meadows and woods belonging to wealthy families.

Like most villages, Highfield had its 'characters'. One often mentioned in reminiscences is Charlie Bush, who was a carter, organ-blower and bellringer at the turn of the century. He is remembered for the red handkerchief with which he mopped his face after ringing the church bell for half an hour before a service. Charlie rang the bell for almost 50 years and was rewarded with a parish pension.

Some events stick in the memory. The area's royal credentials, if you like, were established when the Royal Southampton Horticultural Society set up at Westwood Park; their 1902 fête celebrated Edward VII's coronation. There were Royal visits, too. University College had the flags out for the Prince of Wales, later Edward VIII, who toured the town in June 1924, when he came to open the floating dry dock. A decorative arch spanned Portswood Junction for the occasion.

The Duke of York (later George VI) opened Highfield Hall, the new College hostel for women students, on 1 July 1930. From Stag Gates to Highfield Road children from all the elementary schools of the town lined up, while from the Highfield Road turning to the hostel in Omdurman Road secondary-school children continued the human avenue, each waving a streamer of red, white or blue. Other Royal visitors have included Princess Alice and Princess Beatrice, both of whom came to Highfield in the 1920s.

Highfield folk have seen much but have suffered fewer changes than many other suburbs. Street names have sometimes been altered. Portswood Back Lane became Church Lane and University Road, and Chaplin Street (formerly Chapel Street, it was renamed after a local notable) turned into Roselands Gardens, after Kimber's old house Roselands.

Generally, the changes have been kindly. In a competition to name Southampton's prettiest area Highfield would undoubtedly win hands down.

Monica Brown, whose memories led us up many interesting avenues of research.

Imagine Portswood Green, in the heart of the countryside. What a contrast with today's busy Portswood shopping centre! Come back in time to the end of the eighteenth century when, behind the present Kwik Save food store, there stood an elegant mansion called Portswood Lodge (later renamed Portswood House) which fronted Portswood Road and had grounds stretching back to Brookvale Road. Here lived the inventor of the circular saw, Walter Taylor, who had made his fortune from producing wooden pulley blocks for the Navy.

Two artists, Jonathan Spilsbury and his daughter Maria, who were friends of the Taylors, settled for a while as their neighbours at Portswood Green.

Maria, later to marry Taylor's son John, busied herself sketching 'rural scenes' in the Highfield area while her father sought orders for the then fashionable miniatures. A letter from Mr Spilsbury at that time (1798) provides in a few words a vivid picture of affluent life during the reign of George III:

> Maria thinks if we meet with encouragement here we may spend our Summers here and Winters in Town. Our journey down and up, if we travelled in a P. Chair, would not be ten pounds per Annum and I think would contribute much to our Health, perhaps be a means of prolonging our Life.

(Could 'P. Chair' be a misreading of 'P. Chaise', i.e. 'Post-chaise', on the part of Ruth Young, the Spilsburys' biographer?)

Walter Taylor died in 1803. One of the mansion's later occupants was Walter Perkins, who changed the name from Portswood Lodge to Portswood House, which confusingly had been the name of a demolished stately home on the other side of Portswood Road.

In 1841 the house and 32 acres of land was put up for letting.

A newspaper advert described it as being 'within an easy distance of three packs of Fox hounds'. Nowadays the packs have gone but not the still abundant quarry! Walter Taylor's old home remained until 1923 as a reminder of Georgian values, even though its frontage had been taken over a decade previously by shops, the Palladium cinema and a library.

Left: *Jonathan Spilsbury. A self-portrait.*
Right: *Maria Spilsbury. A self-portrait painted when the artist was sixteen.*

This painting of a New Year's Day feast at Walter Taylor's Portswood House school for his workers' children is interesting because it includes the earliest depiction of a black person in Southampton. It was fashionable early in the nineteenth century for wealthy people to have a black slave. The one shown here, Tony, was a faithful servant to the Taylors for many years. The painting is attributed by Tudor House Museum (where it reposes) to Mrs Augusta Taylor, but other sources say the artist was Maria Taylor, the Taylors' daughter-in-law.

3 - 'Nob Hill'

In Victorian times, beyond the farmland up the gentle hill from Portswood, and mostly facing the eastern side of the Common, stood a number of houses owned by the gentry and a handful of cottages occupied by the equally respectable, if less well-off. This was Highfield's 'Nob Hill'.

An 1897 map shows Ivy Bank to the north and Oak Mount to the south (both houses survive). The southernmost was Highfield House, a substantial, reputedly Georgian property. No illustration or photograph of it can be traced, though it was pulled down as late as 1929 to make way for a block of flats at the corner of Oakmount Avenue and Westbourne Crescent. However, its 'Gothick' lodge-house remains to delight the eye at the top of Oakmount Avenue.

Admirals favoured the house in the nineteenth century, first Vice-Admiral Foote, then Rear-Admiral Morier, who was succeeded by William Ogden and his daughter. The year 1883 brought a new name to the street directory when tailor and outfitter James Ireland made it his residence.

Going north, the map shows Highfield Cottage (not, one supposes, a cottage in the usual modest sense) and Highfield Uplands, for many years associated with the wealthy McCalmont family who figure elsewhere in this book.

A local magistrate and retired army officer, Major Alexander Corse-Scott, married one of the McCalmonts' daughters. The couple lived with Mrs McCalmont at Uplands in the closing years of the century, but in 1913 it was on the market. The demolition men moved in and the new Taunton's School was later built on the site.

Interesting developments also affected the adjoining property, Heather Deane, where Colonel Bridges barked orders in the nineties. Occupying the frontage in

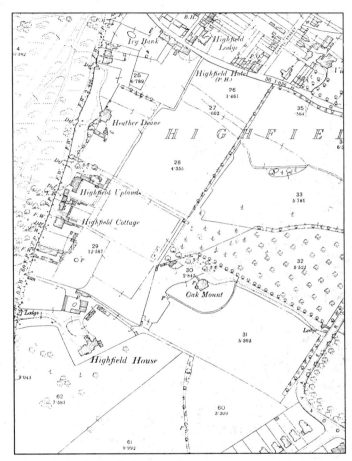

Part of the 1897 Ordnance Survey map showing the residences of Highfield's 'Nob Hill' gentry, including Highfield House, Oak Mount, Highfield Uplands, Heather Deane (later Highfield Mansions and the first Highfield Hall), Ivy Bank and Highfield Lodge.

Back view of Highfield Mansions during its time as a hotel. From a brochure in the possession of Southampton collector Bill White.

Highfield Road between Khartoum and Omdurman roads, it later underwent a name-change to Highfield Mansions, though the old name lives on in nearby Heatherdeane Road. An entrepreneur, Robert Horsley Gudgeon, ran the house as a hotel, but the venture, in the early years of the century, was short-lived.

Because of a legal technicality the house stood empty for some years, but in 1913 was leased by Dr Alex Hill, principal of University College. Under another new name, Highfield Hall, it became his private residence and a students' hostel. During the war it served as a Red Cross Hospital, but in 1930 a new women's hall of residence, also called Highfield Hall, was opened in the grounds. By 1932 the old building had been demolished.

The 'upstairs, downstairs' face of Highfield was changing....

New Year's Eve, 1952. Photographed from the Common end of Oakmount Avenue, this snowscape shows (left) the old lodge of Highfield House.

4 – Death at the Uplands

The McCalmonts of Highfield were well off and well connected. Earls and lords were numbered among their relatives. But in less than a couple of years, underlining the truth that death is no respecter of wealth or position, two distinguished scions of this village 'squirearchy' met their Maker at the ages of 26 and 34 respectively.

They were the sons of the Revd Thomas McCalmont, who seems to have been content not to exercise his Holy Orders but merely to lead the life of a country gentleman. His boys, however, both made their mark locally and, in one case, nationally.

The family came over from Ireland and settled in Highfield's upper reaches. The 1861 Post Office Directory lists Thomas as living at The Rosaries (a house called The Rosary elsewhere), but four years later his address is given as Uplands. Over the years there has been speculation about the change. Uplands was perhaps a more suitable name for a Church of England cleric.

The clergyman's third son, Alfred, was elected Mayor of Southampton in 1877, making him probably the youngest mayor of any town in the country. He was only 26. A year later he was dead, having succumbed to congestion of the brain and typhoid fever.

The family story continued on its melancholy way less than two years later, when Alfred's elder brother Frederick, a barrister and local alderman, died at 34. He had spent the day on a friend's yacht and afterwards dined with him at the Dolphin Hotel, having decided beforehand to spend the night at Radley's Hotel in Oxford Street. Next morning he was found dead there.

At first it was thought that he had taken an overdose of chloral (he took it for insomnia) but an autopsy revealed that his heart and kidneys were diseased.

There are two stained-glass windows in Highfield Church dedicated to the memory of the Revd Thomas McCalmont and his Highfield-born sons Frederick and Alfred, and paid for 'by 312 of their friends'.

Frederick is also remembered among historians because he compiled and published the still useful *Parliamentary Poll Book*, recording the polls in all the constituencies of the country from 1832 to 1879.

Frederick McCalmont wasn't the only well-known person to die at Radley's (later the Royal Mail House). The American humorist Artemus Ward breathed his last there on 6 March 1867.

Local politicians Frederick (left) and Alfred McCalmont. Their uncle, Earl Cairns, was Lord Chancellor.

5 - 'A Pretty Village Church'

In his 1852 guidebook *A Picture of Southampton*, that multi-talented artist, architect and general 'Renaissance man' Philip Brannon wrote: 'Christ Church is a pretty village church, in plain decorated style, wonderfully correct in the revival of Gothic architecture, and is situated in the delightfully rural village of Portswood.'

At that time 'Christ Church, Portswood, commonly

An early photograph of Highfield Church showing the wooden fence round the churchyard which was later replaced by a wall. Note, to the left, the narrowness of Highfield Lane, then a dusty path shaded by overhanging trees.

called Highfield Church' (as an earlier noticeboard describes it) was only half a dozen years old. It was a time when Highfield Lane really was a lane, with (to quote the centenary brochure of 1947) 'overhanging hedges almost like a tunnel in parts'.

The joint architect of the church, which began as a chapel of ease in the parish of South Stoneham, was Joshua Brandon who, like the distinguished sons of the building's principal benefactor, 'Squire' McCalmont, was cut off in his prime, dying at 25 in 1847. He is buried in the church he was destined never to see completed.

Not all the changes proposed over the ensuing years were made without controversy. When, in 1861, it was proposed to enlarge the organ, its donor, the wealthy Thomas McCalmont, was distinctly miffed. The instrument, he declared, should be placed at the Bishop's disposal for use in another church 'where the congregation would appreciate it'! The storm blew over.

The still highly popular church, where thousands have worshipped for over a century and a half, drew a packed congregation on Sunday, 13 February 1955 to welcome a not unfamiliar visitor: the Bishop of

Highfield Church c. 1900. The original chancel has been extended and trees dominate the churchyard.

Lichfield, who from 1936 until 1943, as the Revd A.S. Reeve, was Vicar of Highfield.

In his address he recalled the Saturday night before the first Sunday in Lent in 1941 when eight bombs fell around the church – miraculously, without hitting it. There was damage, true, but the eight o'clock service was held the following morning none the less. The purpose of the Bishop's visit was to dedicate a porch in memory of the eminent Highfield resident Sir Sidney Kimber.

The church hasn't always won approval for its design (some clergymen complained that pillars blocked the view from the pulpit), but one expert praised its lively gargoyles: 'unusually large and mock-fearsome beasts'.

The ringing-in of 1997 marked a highly important anniversary in the history of Christ Church, Portswood, always known as Highfield Church: its 150th. It was to be a year of exhibitions and special services, and everybody in the parish was promised an anniversary mug.

Though not the only church in the parish – the popular evangelical Portswood Church, on the 'Broadway' side of Portswood Road, just scrapes into the parish map – Christ Church is its almost literal centre, sacred and secular as well as geographical.

The congregation, and around 800 people attend services every Sunday, is constantly changing. This is due to two main factors: the job mobility of the professional classes who choose to live in this, let's face it, up-market area, and of course the presence within the parish boundaries of the ever-developing university.

The Vicar (the Revd David James) wasn't unaware of the student impact when he arrived in 1990, for at the end of the 1960s, when he taught chemistry at the university, he was a member of the congregation, and he returned to Highfield as a curate (1973–76) before taking up his present appointment.

A staff just under double figures ensures that the 5,707 souls Christ Church serves are looked after socially as well as spiritually. Among its many organisations are youth and drama groups and clubs for toddlers and carers. There's even a cricket team.

It's not so surprising, bearing in mind its strong support, that this 'low' church with high aims should prove vocationally fruitful: most years people from Highfield are ordained to serve God throughout the land. The parish church has always been evangelically

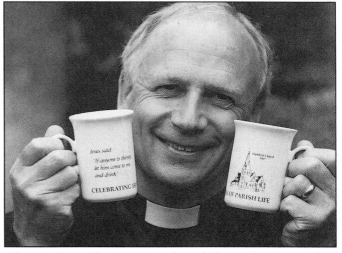

The Revd David James: member of the congregation, then curate and now Vicar of Highfield Church

active, regularly sending missionaries abroad and even helping to boost other churches in the area by giving them that valuable resource: people.

Highfield churchgoers support, among others, a dermatologist in Tanzania, and are rallying to the cause of Indian land rights in South America. It all seems a long way from the snooty 1920s, when Highfield's Mothers' Union decided not to admit working-class members to its committee.

The anniversary celebrations planned for the big month, September, had as their centrepiece a City of Southampton Society Open Day, when both the church and its Institute were chosen as examples of a Victorian church and an Edwardian church centre.

A picture of Highfield Church Institute, taken in the days before Highfield Lane was a made-up road. The church centre has changed little externally, but inside it's a different story.

7 – Babbling Brooks in Shady Nooks

The late Lawrence Burgess, the librarian whose wide knowledge illuminated many an excursion of the Friends of Old Southampton, took a particular interest in the waterways of his city. In 1968 the Friends published the results of his researches in a fascinating paper, 'The Streams and Watercourses of Southampton', in which he writes about Highfield's streams.

The first, he tells us, rises at the edge of the Common a hundred yards south of the Highfield Lane–Highfield

The ornamental pool in Highfield Close

Road junction and is culverted under Nile Road and Heatherdeane Road.

The architect of the beautiful Uplands Estate, Herbert Collins, made use of it 'as a village green amenity in the transit of Orchards Way' and, even more imaginatively, fed it into 'the spectacular ornamental pool in Highfield Close'. The stream crosses Portswood Road, then picks up a tributary that shapes the line of the appropriately named Brookvale Road.

It was Mr Burgess's belief that another Highfield 'streamlet' and its two successors were connected to a fishpond and canal constructed by the canons of St Denys. The first, one and three-quarter miles long, rises in Bassett and crosses the north-east corner of the Common into the University gardens. Then it enters that delightful little bird sanctuary behind Glebe Court (another green wheeze from Mr Collins) and reaches Church Lane before passing domestic flower borders and running under Church Lane and Shaftesbury Avenue on its way to the Itchen.

It may have been just a 'streamlet' to our Mr Burgess, but it was given the grandiose title of Highfield River on a fairly recent map. However, 'Townsman' (E.A. Mitchell), author of the pre-war *Echo's* 'Occasional Notes', wrote that it bore no name. After running across the north-east corner of the Common, 'at what was once a very picturesque spot', it passed under a wooden bridge, skirted the brickfields which preceded the present university and went under Church Lane 'in the roadway of which it once formed a pond'.

The canal mentioned earlier apparently tapped another stream rising between Kitchener Road and Bowden Lane. Then there is the Boundary Brook which rises just over the Highfield border in Burgess Road. Its valley lies between Broadlands Road on one side and Granby Grove/Sirdar Road on the other. Finally, Mr Burgess tells us that a tiny, 50-yard stream alongside what was once Botany Department in the university grounds has the distinction of being represented on the sixteenth-century town map.

The 'Highfield River' passes through the garden of John and Julia Slade in Shaftesbury Avenue.

Roselands, which gave its name to that rather charming Highfield backwater, Roselands Gardens, with its forks and nooks and hints of a rural past, may not have counted as one of the village's 'big houses', but it makes up for its modest size by its history of domiciling a succession of remarkable self-made men. The first of these was the man who built it, Richard Kimber, a schoolmaster-turned-brickmaker

Roselands (in what was then Chaplin Street) at the turn of the century

Sir Sidney Kimber

the visionary who saw to it that his dreams of a civic centre and a sports centre were realised, Sidney was eventually knighted for his services.

'The old so-and-so', Labour dubbed him. His view of the opposing party was light-hearted. 'Now then, behave yourself, Mollie,' he would say to Mrs Mary O'Higgins, wagging his finger, as she vented her Irish temper at him. Even his detractors had a grudging respect for the far-sighted boss of the borough.

In 1901 Sidney, who later moved to another Highfield house, the now demolished Oakdene in Welbeck Avenue, sold Roselands to the equally colourful William Bennett, who in 1885 established the first canteen inside Southampton Docks. Bennett's enterprise led to several more canteens, a restaurant for liner passengers and sightseers, a slaughterhouse, a pig farm and property development.

Like William Bennett, who was the son of a St Mary's alehouse keeper, Charlie Knott came from a tough background in downtown Southampton. Born into dockland poverty in 1891, Charlie, through dint of hard work and business acumen, moved up-market to Roselands. 'Sell anything except the wife and kids,' he joked.

A fish-shop entrepreneur, he invested in trawler companies, supplying fish 'from trawler to customer'. Charlie's favourite sport was coursing. His son, the former Hampshire cricketer C.J. Knott, who lives in Highfield Lane at an appropriate address (The Wickets), recalls exercising greyhounds as a lad when the family were living at Roselands. Charlie is famed as the founder of the Stadium and the pre-war Sportsdrome and as a promoter not only of greyhounds but of speedway, ice- and roller-skating and many other sports. What a showman!

whose business prospered on a site now occupied by university buildings. But it was Richard's son Sidney who made the name Kimber memorable.

The nearest British equivalent to an American political boss, Sidney strode the first decades of this century like a Colossus, invariably getting his own way and ignoring any opposition. Tory leader, First World War Mayor and

9 – A Link with a Rural Past

With the demolition in 1997 of a former farm cottage, No. 47 Roselands Gardens, previously 23 Chaplin Street, one of the last remaining links with Highfield's rural past disappeared. Margaret ('Patsy') Goodall remembers living next door to it as a small child nearly 70 years ago:

It was a very old cottage, thatched, and with very long gardens both back and front. There were tiny box hedges surrounding small square plots, with lots of flowers in the front garden and an old apple tree.

I was only a child of four when, in the late 1920s, we came to live next door to the elderly couple.

They were very 'countrified', both in their dress and language. They were very kind and always welcomed me into their house and garden. Their name was Small.

The house, to me as a child, was wonderful. It was full of strange smells: of snuff, 'baccy, boiled bacon, cabbage, apples and mustiness, all at the same time.

Patsy, aged four, with Mrs Small

And Mrs Goodall today

The Smalls' cottage in later years

Semi-detached houses replaced the old cottage in 1997.

I was allowed to wander as I pleased. Outside the back door there was a water butt with smelly rainwater, ages old, and apples bobbing on the surface.

There was a long, long garden at the back which dipped down quite low and then rose to a high plateau at the top. The garden had a hedge around it and a seat in the centre. I would love to run up and down the garden path and sit on the seat at the top. Old George – 'Jarge', his wife called him – used to say to my mother: 'She do run like the wind.'

'Jarge' had lots of vegetables and fruit trees in his back garden and would put shovels of manure on the vegetables – 'To make them grow', he told me. I thought it would be a good idea to put some in my shoes! This I did, and put so much in I could hardly walk. When all was finally revealed I was a figure of fun for a long time.

Mrs Goodall, who now lives in Portswood, remembers the old cottage and its occupants with nostalgia and love. She recalls, too, that the old place had seen tragedy, for it was from the apple tree in the front garden that 'Jarge', arthritic and nearly blind, hanged himself in later years.

The building lost much of its rustic charm when the thatch was replaced by tiles and new windows and doors were put in. Now a modern housing development on the site further illustrates the march of 'progress'.

10 – The Story of a Village School

The history of Highfield Church of England School goes back to 1846 with a deed of covenant stating that Stephen Ram of Ramfort, County Wexford:

granted and conveyed two perches of land out of a piece named Small Gains Field and facing Back Lane to the minister and churchwardens of South Stoneham and their successors for a school for the education of children in the labouring, manufacturing and other poorer classes in the parish of Stoneham and as a residence for the schoolmaster or schoolmistress.

Ram lived at one of the village's 'big houses', Portswood Lodge (later Portswood House). Like the wealthy McCalmonts who lived at the other end of Highfield, Ram was of Irish origin. Small Gains Field formed part of his estate. Back Lane is now known as Church Lane.

The school, two years younger than the church it adjoined, was opened in 1849 and originally consisted of the master's house, later occupied by the verger, and one classroom. Other classrooms were added as Highfield grew and became an independent parish. An extract from a Victorian logbook reminds us of the rural place Highfield once was: '1869 – School short –

Pupils of Standard Five at Highfield School gathered for this photograph in 1913.

The old Highfield School, photographed in March, 1970

haymaking'. At which point we repeat the old poser: does the name Highfield derive from 'Hayfield'?

Originally the school was maintained by 'school pence', subscriptions and government grants.

Of all the headmasters it has had, Harry Leggett is the one who seems to have evoked the fondest memories. He taught there for 38 years, for 22 as head, retiring in 1957. During the Second World War, when lessons were held in air-raid shelters during daylight raids, Mr Leggett was awarded the MBE for leading an ARP wardens' rescue of a woman trapped in a bombed house.

A new epoch for the school began in 1970 when juniors from the Primary (Aided) School marched from the old Church Lane premises to architect Colin Hewett's attractively designed new school building in Hawthorn Road.

At the time of the move the Infants were known as

The late 1950s: Highfield School pupils next to the huts on what locals still call 'the Little Common' (the Common's eastern side).

'hutites' because they had occupied four wartime huts on the Common. These had served as 'temporary' school buildings for 25 years! The old school was refurbished to accommodate the First School and the huts were demolished.

No mention of the school would be complete without some reference to Mollie Bennett, a 'Miss Chips' who died aged 101 in 1983. Her father, John, was the headmaster and for the first 20 years of her life Mollie lived at the school house, until he died in 1901. She spent her entire teaching career at the school, retiring in 1946 after 46 years. In 1985 two hornbeam trees were planted in her memory near the Highfield Lane–Cranford Way junction.

Alderman Kathy Johnson at the controls as school huts are demolished in 1970

11 – Taunton's – The Name Lives On

In 1993, Taunton's, the grammar school turned sixth-form college, ended close on 70 years' association with Highfield when Richard Taunton College (as it had become) amalgamated with Hill College in Upper Shirley and moved there. Richard Taunton, the old wine importer and merchant whose somewhat dubious fortune led to the bequest that founded the original school, would be pleased to know that his name lives on as Taunton's College.

The handsome premises where generations of Southampton schoolboys studied now forms part of the University's Avenue Campus.

Like some of the schoolboys who later benefited from his munificence, Richard Taunton, a true-born Sotonian and a cousin of the hymnwriter Isaac Watts, 'blotted his copybook' when, together with the Mayor, he was accused of political chicanery. It was said that he tried to get a candidate elected to Parliament by attempting to disenfranchise electors. The election result was overturned.

Taunton derived part of his fortune from the spoils of war. In 1745 two privateers of which he was part-owner raided three French ships and captured their cargo of silver and gold. In peacetime such activity would have been considered piracy.

Taunton's was founded in 1752, the benefactor's bequest enabling 20 boys to be taught reading, writing, arithmetic and navigation 'to fit them for the sea', though the nautical emphasis was eventually dropped. The school, initially in Windsor Terrace, was well established by 1865 when purpose-built premises opened in New Road. In 1875 it became Taunton's Trade School, a title which lasted until 1910, when it became a public secondary school.

By the Edwardian era Taunton's School had grown so

Richard Taunton

much that its administrators proposed new school buildings for 600 boys. Early in 1913 the borough council were told that a piece of land – Highfield Uplands – had been purchased by W.F.G. Spranger, chairman of the governors, who offered to sell it to the

Taunton's School. The building in Highfield Road became a sixth-form college before being taken over by the university.

RN Leading Seaman Jack Mantle, an Old Tauntonian, who won a posthumous VC in the Second World War.

council, provided that it be used for the new Taunton's School. This was agreed, but the outbreak of war and other factors delayed the laying of the foundation stone until 1925.

Taunton's went on thriving, developing in its new role as a sixth-form college from 1967.

It has had famous as well as infamous pupils, including Benny Hill, Ken Russell, John Stonehouse and some luminaries who aren't, or weren't, household names like Lord Hollick, chairman of Meridian TV, and Atomic Energy Authority executive Sir Donald Perrott.

It had a particularly famous English teacher in Dr H.M. King (later Lord Maybray King), who became a Southampton MP and later Speaker of the House of Commons.

The first cricket match to be played on the playing fields of what would become the 'new' Taunton's School. The spire of Highfield Church can be seen in the distance.

What with the University, Taunton's, Highfield and Portswood Schools and a clutch of private establishments, Highfield seems always to have been well catered for in the field of education.

Overlooking the 'rec' is Portswood School, like High- field's much loved. The complex of buildings seems dauntingly vast for a mere primary school, but this reflects the changed needs of the area.

When the foundation stone of Portswood Elementary School (formerly a temporary Board school) was laid on

Part of the Portswood School complex

27 June 1904, it was stated that it would accommodate 360 boys, 360 girls and 400 infants.

The schools along the southern parish boundary were for the well-to-do. In the early decades of the century there was New College, on the corner of Brookvale Road and Westwood Road, 'for the daughters of professional men'. It was run by the formidable Miss Agnes Allnutt, known as 'The Nutt', whose stern glances were much feared, not least by local historian-to-be Elsie Sandell.

Another establishment for girls, St Winifred's, moved to Westwood Road after its Archers Road premises were blitzed. Founded in 1880, it claimed to be the city's oldest private independent school, and is still going strong.

With the expansion to Townhill Park House, Gregg School's Winn Road premises now cater for the senior pupils.

One long-lived Highfield school is no more. Oakmount, in Brookvale Road, closed in 1989. In April of that year Mr Joseph Savage, headmaster of the 175-

Oakmount: the house

pupil boys' prep school for 32 years, told the Press that the owners had decided not to renew the twelve-year lease on the site.

The old mansion, built in 1850 as a 'gentleman's residence' before becoming a school in 1907, was put on the market together with its grounds. This has resulted in the present attractive estate on the site in which the house, albeit modernised to suit late-twentieth-century occupation, has been retained. So have the carriage drive and lodge.

Other private schools included Ivydene, Ravenscroft Preparatory School for Girls (which closed in the late Twenties) and Charminster Preparatory School. Further education was represented at the Portswood end of Highfield Lane, where the the Southampton School of Commerce was situated.

13 – The Portswood House Estate

An etching in the *Illustrated London News* of 27 July 1844 depicts the grounds of Portswood Lodge (later House) being used for the Royal Agricultural Show. In her well-researched booklet, 'The Portswood House Estate and the Portswood Residents' Gardens', Sylvia Landsberg states that the 16-acre showground must have extended from Portswood Road to approximately the line of Brookvale Road, occupying all the land now covered by the Residents' Garden and its perimeter plots and all the Abbott's Way plots, but not

The Residents' Garden pavilion. Time has made it less Picturesque!

the area known as the Meadow – like the garden, 'for subscribers only'.

The Abbott referred to in the name Abbotts Way was one Captain Abbott, leaseholder of Portswood House in the 1840s. Although he was remembered when the estate was developed for housing in the following century, it wasn't the first time his name had been attached to the landscape: the 32-acre area he leased was known as Abbott's Park. After the captain's death in 1857 Portswood Lodge was often empty. Walter Perkins bought it in 1875 and changed its name.

When he in turn died, in 1907, a family company, the chairman of which was Walter's son-in-law Sir Russell Bencraft (see 'A Highfield "Who Was Who"', on page 71), made plans to develop the estate. Sylvia Landsberg tells us that seventeen houses had been built by 1914. The bulk appeared in the 1920s and a few in the 1930s, then there was 'a subsequent trickle'.

Not an architecturally organic whole like Herbert Collins' adjoining 'garden city' development, the Perkins estate was a mixture of styles but none the less attractive for that. One of its most interesting features is the Residents' Garden, complete with tennis courts and a pavilion which has, or rather had, a suggestion of 'cottage ornée' about it. Another amenity is the Meadow, an unusually rural feature to find in the middle of a city; in the First and Second World Wars it switched patriotically to allotments.

In 1910 an agreement was drafted and subscriptions

The gates to the Residents' Gardens in Abbotts Way. They were formerly at Portswood House.

were called for from those who wanted to use the garden or play games. The Whithedswood Company which had launched the estate handed over administration to a group of trustees in the spring of 1930.

The garden regulations listed in 1931 sound rather intimidating. For example: 'Any person recovering from an infectious disease is prohibited from entering the garden,' and, underlining the middle-class ambience: 'Persons left in charge of any house are expressly prohibited from going into the garden, and servants unless in attendance on the occupiers.'

14 - Herbert Collins: A Man of Vision

The Uplands Estate has been justifiably described as the jewel in the crown of the architect Herbert Collins (1885–1975). With its symmetry, sylvan setting and beautiful simplicity, it certainly rivals any of his other grand designs. Collins' crown jewel is Highfield's, too.

The great man's biographer and fellow architect, Robert Williams, occupant of a Collins house in another

'England, home and beauty': the Uplands Estate in the 1920s, with Orchards Way under construction below Highfield Close

Herbert Collins, architectural visionary and man of peace

part of the city, describes the estate's 200 houses and flats, built mainly between 1922 and 1936, as 'grouped in short terraces around small greens, or set informally along winding grass-bordered roads, amid carefully preserved trees and an existing stream'.

Collins' elegant and simple Georgian style, best complemented by blossomy spring or early summer, conjures up a peaceful vision, befitting a man who served for decades in the cause of peace. The overall effect is an echo of the garden city movement, so it comes as no surprise to learn that the architect was not only a friend of Sir Ebenezer Howard, its founder, but also a director of the Welwyn Garden City company. In 1921 Collins made his own proposals for a – sadly unrealised – garden city around Marchwood.

The proximity of the estate to the University has meant that its half a dozen roads have become honorary 'olive groves of Academe'. Many professors

Before the Second World War Herbert Collins designed a wrought-iron gateway to a block of flats in Highfield Lane. The gates, melted down as part of the war effort, were replaced in 1987 by a centenary gate dedicated to his memory. With Highfield turning out 'en fête' for the occasion, Herbert Collins' daughter Julie Ozwell officially opened it, and the Mayor for that year, Jack Candy, unveiled a memorial plaque.

have moved into the highly desirable Collins houses.

Some of their neighbours have in one sense been bigger than the houses they occupied, including old salts like Captain Sir Benjamin Chave, the docks boss Reg Biddle, local education chief Frank Freeman and Don Portbury, the novelist, as well as solicitors, the occasional retired colonel and, of course, in one of the Brookvale Road houses he designed, H.C. himself.

Highfielders were afforded considerable amusement in the postwar years when one of Mr Collins' relatives placed an old Southampton tram (they were withdrawn from service in 1949) on the vacant plot next to his house. It has been replaced by another of the architect's creations, the Vicarage.

15 – When Horses Pulled the Trams

In his history of Southampton tramways Martin Petch declares: 'No enthusiasts' trip was complete without a visit to the tram shed in Highfield Road'. Certainly, both old and new had an affection for the ramshackle buildings that stood there 20 years after the last Southampton tram had run in December 1949.

The story of public transport at that spot goes back a long way, to the time of horse trams. It was in 1888 that

The old tram sheds, officially called the Permanent Way Depot, shortly before demolition

the Southampton Tramways Company, later the Corporation transport department, bought the freehold of Highfield Stables, which they were already renting for their horses.

Southampton's civil engineer and surveyor Harry Weston noted that the premises included a half-acre of garden ground which could prove valuable for expansion. A commemorative stone on one of the buildings was initialled 'H.L.' and dated 1835; though the initials prompted the guess that they stood for Highfield Lodge, the site was much closer to Highfield Uplands.

The stables consisted of three blocks of double stalls for a total of 31 horses; over them was a spacious loft, and nearby there were a 90-foot long 'bus shed', a smithy and stores, and a cottage occupied by the horse-keeper. The buses referred to were horse omnibuses operated by the company in addition to the trams.

Before the end of the century another building was put up at Highfield to accommodate more omnibuses. The trams historian Frederick Cooper, writing in the *Echo* in 1969, recalled that an oil store was built at Highfield Stables in 1901 as part of a Corporation experiment with Daimler motor omnibuses. However, because of the unsatisfactory performance of the first one, the order for a further two was cancelled!

In 1904 the electric trams arrived at the Highfield depot, after the tramways were extended from Stag Gates. One line was laid into the shed and the other terminated outside.

The old tram sheds were an eyesore for a couple of decades. In 1969 volunteers from Southampton Sixth Form Union pulled down the old corrugated monstrosities, exposing a brick building which the Union found useful for various functions. Those who remember the site as it used to be would not know it now in its new role as Southampton University's Avenue Campus.

Where once the tram sheds glowered there now stands the 'varsity's archaeology building and a wide road leads to a car park. Curiously, there is (at the time of writing) a site survivor due for closure: a hut used as an Old Tauntonians HQ and until recently by the city's Fo'c'sle folk club.

An unnamed new road leads to a university car park, 1996.

One of the memorable characters of Highfield in the old days was Alfred Pope, who owned and ran the Salisbury Road laundry, properly called the Highfield Hand Laundry (a far cry from the coin-in-the-slot

No prizes for guessing who won this game. Laundryman Alfred Pope, seen here in triplicate, loved taking trick pictures like this one.

launderettes of today – note the word 'hand'.) One of Alfred's grand-daughters, Jean Hawkins, who lived with her parents and sister in Salisbury Road, remembers very well the smell of soap and steam. She told us:

When Henry Groves was building houses in Salisbury Road my grandfather asked him if he would put up a special building in the back garden of No. 2 to house a laundry. I have an agreement signed by them both for a lease of seven years at a yearly rent of £33.16s. It started in 1907 and lasted until 1941.

There were two rooms, the first the wash room, which had two large coppers and two mangles, with overhead wires to dry the clothes, and the second the ironing room. This had a round iron stove on which the irons were heated; each iron was rubbed with wax wrapped in a piece of cloth before ironing. There were also tongs to curl collars, etc.

Alfred Pope once estimated that he had walked the equivalent of twice round the world pushing his hand-cart to deliver and collect laundry.

Before he turned laundryman Alfred was Sir Henry Milner-White's coachman at Bitterne Park's Deepdene. There he met his wife, who was a parlourmaid. They celebrated their golden wedding in 1952.

This enterprising man never went to school and at reading and writing was his own teacher. Keenly interested in photography, he liked experimenting with trick camerawork.

Alfred lived to be 96, an exemplar for hard work. After his laundry days were over he did jobbing gardening until well into his eighties.

Jean Hawkins, of Bitterne, remembers with fondness and amusement her Grandpa Pope.

Education, which seems to have been the village-cum-suburb's principal stock-in-trade in this century, suffered two regrettable interruptions with the advent of the Great War.

The new building of University College (the old Hartley Institution had become recognised as such in 1902) was formally opened on 20 June 1914, but war broke out before lectures could begin there. And half a mile away it had been hoped that the new Taunton's School would soon be rising on the old Highfield Uplands ground.

As war clouds gathered, W.F.G. Spranger, chairman of the governors of Taunton's, entertained the pupils, masters, old boys and governors to tea on the site. But postwar recovery was slow and it wasn't until 1925 that the foundation stone was laid.

The war saw large stretches of the nearby Common covered in military tents and huts. From here and other

Nurses and wounded at the University College military hospital, 1915

camps troops marched down the Avenue to the docks and, in many cases, to their deaths. For the fortunate who survived, however, Highfield proved a healing place.

In 1914 the college authorities handed over their new buildings for use as a military hospital. As the casualties came in from France and Belgium in ever-increasing numbers, wooden huts had to be put up at the rear to deal with the overflow. The huts remained for several years after the war, the college making good use of them until they were eventually replaced by brick buildings.

Death was a regular visitor to the hospital and a mortuary, too, had to be built.

Between Khartoum and Omdurman Roads – names redolent of a previous conflict – there was another hospital. This was in a large country house formerly known as Heather Deane and Highfield Mansions. The Principal of University College, Dr Alex Hill, who had rented it as his family home and as a hall of residence, later changed its name to Highfield Hall. In 1914 Dr Hill lent the property to the Red Cross Society.

In the early part of the war Belgian refugees arrived in large numbers and were accommodated at Tower House in Welbeck Avenue, a building which still stands. Its superintendent was Alderman Sidney Kimber. In November 1918, as Mayor, Kimber announced the end of the war to Southampton's citizens from the balcony of the Audit House, a building which, ironically, would be destroyed in the blitz of 1940.

Belgian refugees at the Tower House, Welbeck Avenue, in October 1914

The 1939–45 conflict brought a grimmer reality to Highfield people than had the Great War. Peter Lewin, then a schoolboy, recalls being under German machine-gun fire on the Common! Here is a memory of another day he would never forget: 'I sang at Morning Prayer as usual on Sunday, March 2, 1941, after the bombing of the church in the night, with rain blowing through empty window frames and streaming through the badly damaged roof.'

Eight bombs were dropped around the church and 700 tiles were dislodged from the roof. The adjoining Institute received a direct hit and the caretaker's house was completely destroyed.

Five months before his damp appearance in the choir, Peter Lewin had seen the falling bombs that wiped out St Barnabas Church, not far away in Lodge Road. The demise of St Barnabas meant that the two parishes were combined for some years.

The Vicar of Highfield, the Revd A. S. Reeve, wrote in his church records that considerable damage was also done to property on the night of 21/22 June 1941. On 15 May 1944, around midnight, many bombs had been dropped on the parish; four people lost their lives, many were injured and numerous houses were made uninhabitable.

Photographs taken during the war years graphically illustrate the amount of bomb damage in the suburb. In one of Ripstone Gardens, beyond a sea of rubble can be seen houses distorted by the blast into twisted shapes reminiscent of early German Expressionist cinema. In

'The village', including the Highfield Hotel, suffered extensive damage in June 1941.

Highfield Lane after a bombing raid in 1941

another wartime picture, of the Highfield Institute, the privacy of a bedroom is exposed by the destruction of a wall.

Another casualty of the bombing was Highfield Hotel, at the corner of Heatherdeane Road and Highfield Lane. Its name dates from 1864. The present pub on the site,

the Highfield, was preceded by a temporary building erected during the postwar years.

Apparently, next door to the Highfield Hotel lived a parrot which had been trained by a serviceman to curse Adolf Hitler. We have been unable to discover whether the bird survived the raid which destroyed the hotel.

Highfield Institute after the raid

As in the Great War, the Common proved a hive of military activity. North of Highfield Avenue was an American camp and to its south a German POW camp.

Residents recall camouflage strung between the trees to cover the Avenue as D-Day approached, and Elsie Sandell, a local historian, wrote: 'We in Westwood Park had a grandstand view of the Allied procession to Normandy, Paris, the Rhine and so to VE Day.'

Salisbury Road residents gather for a tea party to celebrate the end of the war.

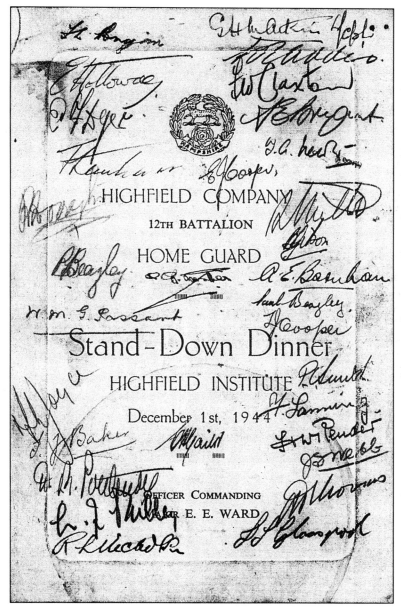

Members of Highfield's 'Dad's Army' signed this programme for their stand-down dinner in December 1944.

19 – Pubs: East Side, West Side

Those unfamiliar with the parish boundaries of Highfield might be surprised to learn that it includes a narrow strip to the east of Portswood Road, stretching from Portswood Avenue in the south to Kent Road in the north, with a church, an eighteenth-century lodge, a cinema turned bingo hall and three of Highfield's modest clutch of pubs.

The first pub locals persist in calling the Belmont, despite its two name changes in less than a decade. It became the Mitre and, more recently, the Pickled Newt,

The Drummond Arms – a real local

the latter a typical example of the increasing silliness of contemporary pub names.

As the road dips down towards Swaythling we come to the more modest Waggoner's Arms, which dates back to the 1860s. Then, as the parish border swings across Portswood Road to skirt Kitchener Road, there is the 'arts' pub Talking Heads, once the Red Lion, which altered not only its name but its pre-karaoke Saturday-night talent contests in favour of drama, blues and other ethnic music.

A real 'local', set in one of the leafy suburb's less elegant spots, is the late-nineteenth-century Drummond Arms at the corner of Somerset Road and Welbeck Avenue.

Generations of university students have quaffed their ales at the former Stile Inn in University Road on the parish's northern frontier. Like the Waggoner's Arms, it dates back to mid-Victorian times. Empty and boarded up in 1989, the pub was gutted in an arson attack the following year and, refurbished, reopened in 1990 as the Hedgehog and Hogshead.

Talking Heads, formerly the Red Lion

The old Highfield Hotel (right) and adjoining houses were destroyed in 1941.

In what is still called Highfield Village stand two pleasant hostelries: the Highfield and the Crown Inn, the first in Highfield Lane and the second, originally a much smaller, nineteenth-century 'watering-hole', just off it in Highcrown Street. When the Crown's licensee, Lil Grant, called 'Time' for the last time in 1980, she could look back on 70 years there, for her parents took over the place as early as 1910. With her departure came refurbishment and, in 1991, a dining-area extension.

In the nineteenth century, when Highcrown Street was known as Crown Street, there were two other pubs in this village heartland: the Orchard Inn and the Rose and Crown.

Tony Gallaher, to whose researches I am indebted, reveals in his publication *Southampton's Inns and Taverns* that there was once another hostelry, on glebe land in Highfield Lane, called the Good Intent, but that was way back in the 1840s.

20 – Lodges and Other Survivors

Highfield abounds in attractive buildings, some of them with an interesting history. Foremost among them is the 'Gothick' – or, if you like, mock-Gothic – lodge-house built in 1776 by General Stibbert, who was also responsible for the first Portswood House. Like the lodge, the long-demolished mansion was castellated, stuccoed and turreted.

It is delightful that such a charming conceit as No. 324

The 'Gothick' lodge in Portswood Road, out of place in a modern urban landscape

Portswood Road (to give the lodge's correct address) should have survived into the late twentieth century.

Another lodge-house of similar charm is the one facing the Common at the top of Oakmount Avenue (No. 38). It served Highfield House, pulled down over 60 years ago to make way for housing. This lodge, younger than the one previously mentioned, was built at a time when the fashion for the so-called Picturesque was on the wane.

No. 38 has changed hands quite a lot over the years and at the time of writing was on the market again. So was Brookvale Cottage, in 'The Cut' between Abbotts Way and Highfield Lane. Bearing the date 1865 and the initials 'McC' (presumably for local landowners the McCalmonts), it was formerly a farmhouse and dairy and was at one time called Brookvale Farm.

It's a pretty half-timbered house with unusual brickwork. Pretty, however, is not the description one would apply to the Old Vicarage in Cranford Way, though it is constructed of that attractive buff brick with which

The Old Vicarage – not a pretty sight

many of the older Highfield properties were built, such as a cottage in Highfield Road and a strange garden building in Heatherdeane Road.

A typically Victorian monstrosity built to house the large families prevalent in the last century, the ugly old parsonage seems to have been piled up rather than designed. After the departure of Canon Chitty in 1929 it was sold on the grounds that it was too large and involved too much expense to the incumbent. No. 99 Highfield Lane became the new vicarage.

In contrast to the Old Vicarage, the Highfield Institute is architecturally pleasing, having changed more internally than externally over the years. When the Institute celebrated its golden jubilee in 1957 there were reminders of the 1907 opening on view, including the original plans and the collecting box used to reach the target for the cost. The box had been found under the stage only a day or so previously.

Present on the golden day was the Revd M.S. Douglas, who was curate of Highfield when the Institute was planned, built and opened.

The oldest residence in Highfield village, built in 1825: Glen Cottage, later The Glen, now 33 Roselands Gardens

There was always quite a lot to do in Highfield, particularly in the years before and after the Second World War. For one thing, there were two cinemas in the parish, one on either side of Portswood Road.

The Palladium at Portswood Junction opened in 1913 and was the first building to go up on what had been part of the old Portswood House estate. It had a good innings, finally succumbing to the then prevalent cinema fate of 'death by television' on 3 May 1958. There's a supermarket there now.

The Broadway was luckier. Like the Atherley over in Shirley, the building (quite an attractive one) survived by courtesy of bingo. Ken Russell's favourite haunt,

The Highfield Bowling Club, now vanished

The Palladium cinema and (right) the Library

turreted and castellated without and boasting Arthurian decor within, opened in June 1930, and died as a cinema in October 1963.

Next door to the Palladium site is Portswood Library, a pleasant-looking compact building rightly loved by its patrons, which opened in 1913. City boss Sidney Kimber boasted in his memoirs that for it he had bought '58 feet at £10 per foot frontage'.

Clubs of varying types stipple the local landscape, one of the most interesting of which is 'Dom Polski', or Polish Home, founded by Polish expatriates in 1963 in a Portswood Road building which had previously been, among other things, a dancing school. They worked in parties of 20 to 40 each evening for seven months to get it ready.

As some clubs thrive, others die. One of the saddest

losses was the old Highfield Bowling Club, hidden behind a row of houses in Salisbury Road. Founded in 1923, it fell to the bulldozers in 1988. A University electronics department now stands where the club's 50 members played.

Many organisations have met over the years at the Albany in Winn Road (formerly the Stafford House Hotel) and at what is now the County Hotel, on the corner of Highfield Lane and Shaftesbury Avenue.

The Albany, dating from 1951, was sold for housing development in 1988 but what was formerly known as the Cotswold Hotel, then as the Moat House, survives under its latest name. The city's post-war jazz developments began here when Southampton Rhythm Club held its weekly meetings at the Cotswold.

Finally, a word about the 14th Highfield Scout Troop, which was officially registered as early as March 1909, and is still going strong.

The Southampton Rifle Club at target practice in Highfield in September 1914

22 – Before the University

The huge University of Southampton, which at the time of writing welcomes about 3,500 students each year and has been spreading its tentacles beyond its home base of Highfield, had its humble origins in the life, or rather death, of a strange sexual revolutionary named Henry Robertson Hartley (1777–1850), whose ambition was to set up his own harem.

The son of a wine merchant, Hartley left £103,000 to Southampton Corporation on condition that it employed:

the interest, dividends and annual proceeds thereof in such manner as might best promote the study and

advancement of the sciences of Natural History, Astronomy, Antiquities, Classical and Oriental Literature in the town, such as by forming a Public Library, Botanic Gardens, Observatory, and collections of objects with the above sciences.

The city fathers burnt their benefactor's 'obscene and blasphemous' manuscripts, but put up a building in High Street to house his books. Out of this came a college bearing his name: the Hartley Institution. This became, in 1902, the university college that preceded the present university, granted its Royal Charter in 1952.

As described in 'Highfield in the First World War' (see page 47), the new college buildings at Highfield, spring-

The first University College buildings at Highfield. The one on the left is still under construction.

Highfield Brickworks. University buildings now stand on the site.

ing up on a green fields site off Back Lane (University Road), were formally opened in 1914, but the onset of the Great War meant that they were not used for their intended purpose until peace had returned. The village-cum-suburb became a setting for war hospitals: one at the university college buildings, another at Highfield Hall and a third over the parish border at 'Elmsleigh' in Glen Eyre Road.

The college expanded as the years rolled on and with that expansion came the end of rustic Highfield. Picturesque Church Farm was demolished and an academic bookshop put up in its place. Sir Sidney Kimber's brickyard made way for the Refectory, the Students' Union building and a number of departments.

The longest-serving Principal of University College was Kenneth Vickers (1921–1946), whose motives in laying the foundations for a University of Southampton were, he declared:

to establish a community in which men and women should learn the values of a good life and develop their qualities and characters in order to play a proper part, with truth and righteousness, in the service of their fellow men.

An amusing apocryphal story is told about this rather solemn man. A pre-war Mayor, dictating the invitation list for some civic function or other, declared: 'We must invite Principal Vickers.' The upshot was that Principal Vickers was left out and the leading Anglican clerics of Southampton were invited!

The University College Students' Representative Council of 1904

In the postwar years, and in particular after the granting of full university status in 1952, the former UCS (University College, Southampton) grew tremendously. Not every Highfielder was convinced that it was a

The university gardens in 1959. The Highfield River, which flows through them, continues through the suburb to the Itchen, taking in its stride Glebe Copse, said to be the original Ports Wood. The object in the middle distance is not a sculpture but part of the equipment used by students studying aeronautical engineering.

benevolent growth as private house after private house was acquired for departmental use and familiar landmarks were swept aside by the bulldozers. There were fears that Highfield would be completely trampled by the monster in its midst, but those fears proved mostly groundless.

Nevertheless, the very skyline of what has been described as Southampton's 'broad and sunlit uplands'

Up, up and away. A modern university grows apace.

The Students' Union building in 1962

was altered as the number of students grew and with it their academic and domestic needs. In the academic year 1995/96 the student total was 19,413. No fewer than 3,500 students are welcomed each year into eight faculties. And the expansion continues: work began in June 1996 on a £17 million chemistry building on the Highfield campus.

Sotonians who had expressed concern that the postwar university would keep its culture to itself need not have worried. The Nuffield Theatre, the Turner-Sims Concert Hall and the John Hansard Gallery continue to be what they have always been: a vital part of the city's artistic life.

Both UCS and the University of Southampton have had distinguished academics on their staff and under both titles have produced graduates who subsequently won fame.

The locally born poet Martin Bell was a student at

Southampton in the 1930s and an even more illustrious poet, F.T. Prince, who still resides in Brookvale Road, was Professor of English for many years, having been appointed in 1956.

The former Speaker of the House of Commons, Viscount Tonypandy (George Thomas) graduated in 1929 and Lord St John of Fawsley (then politician-to-be Norman St John Stevas) lectured in law at the university from 1952 to 1953. Other 'politicals' proud of their Alma Mater include the MP Clive Soley, life peer Baroness

The university site during the Second World War. The derelict brickfields can be seen behind the Students' Union.

Hooper and Southampton MPs James Hill, John Denham and Alan Whitehead. Professor of Politics Raymond Plant became, appropriately, Lord Plant of Highfield.

Southampton graduates who found fame in the media include the wildlife presenter Chris Packham, the actor John Nettles and the political correspondent Jon Sopel.

Other 'old boys' are athletes Martin Hyman, Bruce Tulloh and Jon Potter and, perhaps surprisingly, the university can also claim an international model among its former students: Laura Bailey, who graduated in English (as Laura Birks) in 1993.

BENCRAFT, Sir Russell (1858–1943). Remembered as someone with a cheery word for everybody, Dr Bencraft, knighted in 1924, was active in medicine, business, municipal affairs, charitable causes and sport. A Sotonian born and bred, in his early days he played both for the 'Saints' and for Hampshire at cricket.

Oddly, the Christian name rather than the surname of this prewar Winn Road resident lives on in Highfield as the dedicatee of Russell Place. Dr Bencraft, as he then was, had married into the Perkins family of Portswood House (formerly Lodge) and was

Sir Russell Bencraft

chairman of the company which sold off building plots on the site of the old mansion and grounds.

BIDDLE, Sir Reginald (1888–1970). A dapper, super-confident little Channel Islander who lived in Brookvale Road, Reg Biddle guided the destiny of Southampton Docks for 20 years and helped plan the Normandy invasion. First appointed to Southampton in 1907, by 1936 he had risen to the post of Docks and Marine Manager in succession to Sir Eustace Missenden.

For the Normandy invasion he was concerned in operating all ports from the Humber to the Bristol Channel. He was knighted in 1957 and died at the age of 82 while holidaying in his native Jersey.

Sir Reginald Biddle and his wife at the launch of HMS Walkerton

BRIDELL, Frederick Lee (1830–1863). A carpenter's son born in a hovel in downtown Southampton, Bridell had exhibited at the Royal Academy by the age of 21 and is now regarded by many as Southampton's greatest artist. After his death his paintings fetched upwards of £1,000 each.

He was initially contracted to copy Old Masters and the influence of Salvator Rosa, Poussin and the Dutch seen in his later work can probably be traced to this period. By 1858 he was living at Highfield Lodge. That summer, in Rome, he began his masterpiece 'The Colosseum', a subtle study of mist and shadows which is one of 40 of his works in the Southampton Art Gallery collection. By 33 he was dead, having succumbed to TB.

CHAVE, Sir Benjamin (1870–1954). With the death of this genial old salt the port lost one of its last links with the men who learnt their trade before the mast. It was a pity he hadn't lived on until the second folk-song revival; as a young apprentice he sat on the capstan and sang shanties to the men in the rigging. What a welcome visitor to local folk clubs he would have been!

Sir Ben's first command was the *Sabine* – an eight-knot, single-screw vessel lit by oil lamps – in 1914. By 1921 this Southampton-born Old Edwardian had been knighted for his distinguished record of service in the Great War and with the Merchant Navy in general. Sir Ben lived in Glebe Court.

Sir Benjamin Chave

FOOTE, Admiral Edward James (1767–1833). A war-seasoned veteran, he was appointed to the command of the royal yacht *Augusta* in 1803. In 1807, when Captain Foote, as he then was, lived at Highfield House and Jane Austen was living at Castle Square, the two families were friendly.

Jane wrote on 7 January that year:

> He dined with us on Friday and I fear he will not venture again, for the strength of our dinner was a boiled leg of mutton, underdone even for James, and Captain Foote has a particular dislike of underdone mutton, but he was so good-humoured and pleasant that I did not mind his being starved.

Despite the *faux-pas*, the polite sailor gave the Austens a 'most cordial invitation to his house in the country': a vivid reminder of just how rural Highfield was in those days. Made a vice-admiral in 1821 and a KCB in 1831, Admiral Foote died at Highfield House on 23 May 1833.

MITCHELL, Reginald Joseph (1895–1937). Spitfire designer R.J. Mitchell lived at 2 Russell Place. It was a house of his own design and nothing like the cottage on the cliffs depicted in Leslie Howard's film biography of Mitchell, *The First of the Few*. Nor was actor-director Howard anything like the real-life Mitchell.

Howard's Mitchell was typical of the actor's usual characterisations: dreamy, romantic and absent-minded. The real R.J. (according to his son, Dr Gordon Mitchell) was 'forceful, strong, quick-tempered and very much awake all the time'.

R.J. Mitchell

Mitchell hailed originally from Stoke-on-Trent and joined Supermarine at Woolston in 1917. He became their chief engineer and designer, and turned out a succession of successful aircraft, including Schneider Trophy-winning seaplanes. A victim of cancer, he didn't live to see his creation help save his country in the Battle of Britain.

Don Portbury

PORTBURY, Don (b. 1898). Portbury, who was a cashier at the High Street branch of the Midland Bank, had another career, that of novelist. Before the war his *Egypt Lane*, praised by Howard Spring as 'a great achievement', was a best-selling Book of the Month. Three more novels and many short stories followed. Southampton-born Portbury lived at 48 Orchards Way.

Miss Elsie Sandell

SANDELL, Elsie M. (1891–1974). A shipbroker's daughter and a much-loved Southampton historian, Miss Sandell's approach to the subject of her native city's past was pleasingly chatty rather than academically dusty. She was the author of numerous books and a lively speaker, and received an honorary Master of Arts degree from Southampton University in 1967.

In 1970 she moved from her large family home in Winn Road to a 'treetops' flat in Westwood Road. When she died at 83 in the summer of 1974 more than a hundred people attended her funeral at Highfield Church.

WHITWORTH, Lewis Lacey (1892–1995). This Bedford-born long-time resident of Furzedown Road came to Southampton in the mid-1920s to manage a music shop and soon set about organizing a competitive music festival, the need for which had long been recognised.

Southampton's first festival was in 1926. Lewis carried on organising it for the next 48 years and, thanks to his vision, it's still going strong more than 70 years on.

Lewis Whitworth retired to Chilworth with his wife Ethel and died at the great age of 102 at the Lyme Regis home of his son Ivor.

Lewis Whitworth

'The Dip', between Church Lane and Highfield Crescent, at the turn of the century. Flint implements of the Paleolithic period were unearthed here and one is kept in God's House Museum.

Highfield Lane after widening in the Edwardian era

Heatherdeane Road in the 1930s. The old Highfield Hotel can be seen at the top of the road.

Harold and Gladys Jolly in the garden of the Highfield Hotel in 1902. Their parents, Keith and Eva Jolly, were the licensees. At the time of writing Gladys was still alive, aged 97.

Life goes on, despite war and snow: a Lowman's bakery delivery cart in Highfield Avenue in 1942.

The 1950s: spring comes to Abbotts Way.

Highfield Lodge today

Glebe Court, behind which nestles Glebe Copse. The original Ports Wood is now a bird sanctuary.

The Broadway bingo hall, formerly the Broadway cinema (1930–63)

Ploughing land on what later became the site of the Brickworks and is now university land.

Highfield Youth Club members get a taste for Coca Cola in the innocent days of 1962.

Bibliography

Anderson, Alexander, *Hartleyana* (Scottish Academic Press and Southampton University Press, 1987)

Brode, Tony, *The Blitz* (Barry Shurlock & Co., 1977)

Burgess, L.A., *Streams and Watercourses of Southampton* (Friends of Old Southampton Occasional Papers, 1968)

Dedman, Martin, Highfield Church Centenary Brochure, 1947; 'Highfield Church 1847–1977: A Story of Growth, Change and Development'; *Highfield Scout Group Jubilee, 1909–1979*

Gallaher, Tony, *Southampton's Inns and Taverns* (1995)

Hearnshaw, F.J.G. and F. Clarke, *A Short History of Southampton* (Clarendon Press, 1910)

Kimber, Sir Sidney, *Thirty-eight Years of Public Life in Southampton* (1949)

le Faye, Deirdre (ed.), *Jane Austen's Letters* (Oxford Paperbacks, 1997) Landsberg, Sylvia, *The Portswood House Estate and the Portswood Residents' Gardens* (Portswood Residents' Trust, 1997)

Leonard, A.G.K., *Stories of Southampton Streets* (Paul Cave Publications, 1984)

— *More Stories of Southampton Streets* (Paul Cave Publications, 1989)

Mann, John Edgar, *Southampton People* (Ensign Publications, 1989)

Mitchell, Dr Gordon, et al, *R.J. Mitchell* (Nelson & Saunders, 1986)

Petch, Martin, *Southampton Tramways* (Middleton Press, 1994)

Pevsner, Nikolaus and Lloyd, David, *The Buildings of England: Hampshire and the Isle of Wight* (Penguin, 1967)

Rance, Adrian, *Southampton: An Illustrated History* (Milestone Publications, 1986)

Southampton Local Studies Group, *Portswood, a Series of Personal Reminiscences* (1982)

Sweetman, John, *F.L. Bridell, 1830–1863* (Southampton Art Gallery, 1975)

Taunton's School Journals, 1946–58

'Townsman', *Southampton Occasional Notes* (Southern Newspapers, 1938)

Temple Patterson, A., *A History of Southampton 1700-1914* (University of Southampton, Vol. 2, 1971, and Vol. 3, 1975)

— *The University of Southampton* (University of Southampton, 1962)

Ticehurst, Brian and Meachen, Harry, *Pictures of Portswood's Past* (Kingfisher, 1987)

Williams, Robert, *Herbert Collins, Architect and Worker for Peace* (Paul Cave Publications Ltd and the City of Southampton Society, 1985)

Young, Ruth, *Father and Daughter* (Epworth Press, 1952)